IMAGES
of England

ARDWICK

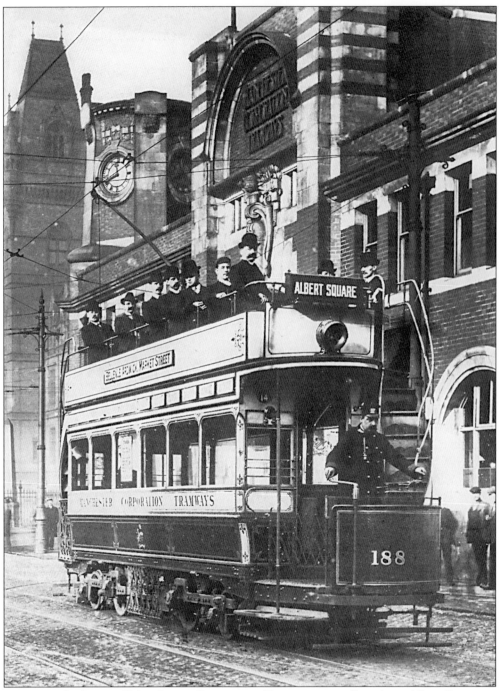

A tram in the livery of Manchester Corporation Tramways, travelling from Albert Square in Manchester city centre to Belle Vue, passes the tram sheds on Hyde Road, Ardwick, *c.* 1900. On the left is the tower of Nicholls Ardwick Hospital (see pp 122-3) on the corner of Devonshire Street North, opposite which is the five-sided clock, a distinctive feature of the tram depot, which would later become the Hyde Road bus depot (see pp 35-36) after the last tram ran in Manchester in 1949.

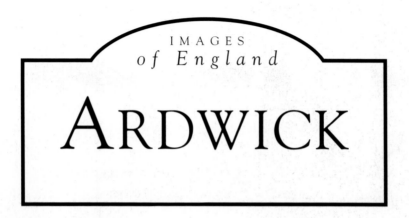

IMAGES
of England

ARDWICK

Compiled by
Jill Cronin and Frank Rhodes

TEMPUS

First published 2002
Copyright © Jill Cronin and Frank Rhodes, 2002

Tempus Publishing Limited
The Mill, Brimscombe Port,
Stroud, Gloucestershire, GL5 2QG

ISBN 0 7524 2473 4

Typesetting and origination by
Tempus Publishing Limited
Printed in Great Britain by
Midway Colour Print, Wiltshire

Dedicated to Les Sutton who spent years recording Ardwick's history.

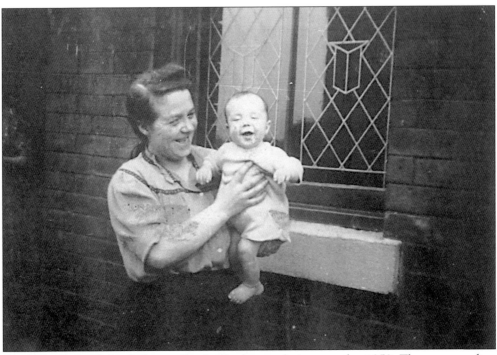

Ethel Rhodes holds her baby son Frank Rhodes, aged nine months, 1950. They are standing outside the home of Ethel's sister, Joan Morris, off Bennett Street in Ardwick.

Contents

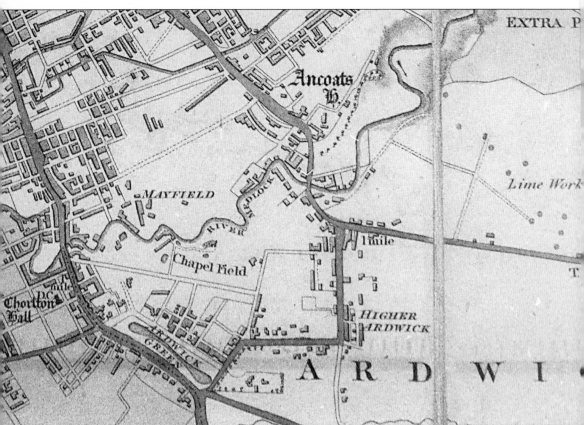

Johnson's map showing Ardwick in 1820. The only areas covered by housing are around Ardwick Green, stretching just north of the green and along Higher, or Upper, Ardwick north towards the River Medlock, which forms for the most part a border between Ancoats and Ardwick. The area of Mayfield north of the river was later to give the area Mayfield station and baths, on opposite sides of the river. Housing follows the line of the main road along Downing (pre-1823 Ardwick) Street into the city centre. There is some occupation around Chapel Field, where later David Moseley's rubber works would retain that name. The south-east corner of the green shows pleasant grounds where Ardwick House (later Hall) lay.

Introduction

Travelling to Manchester city centre from the east, most people today pass through the inner city suburb of Ardwick, probably with scarcely a glance. In 1839, however, Cocker was able to write: 'Ardwick Green is another pleasing suburb, forming an imposing entrance into the town from the south, and ornamented by a fine miniature lake, surrounded by handsome dwellings.' The population and the number of buildings of the township dramatically reduced after the Blitz in the Second World War and after house clearances. The landscape is criss-crossed by rail and road networks, including, since 1967, the Mancunian Way 'flyover'. Ardwick Green however was once populated by the wealthy and famous, whose gracious houses surrounded the green and whose funeral corteges lined up at fashionable Ardwick cemetery. The north part of the township, bounded by the River Medlock, was a hive of industry, providing full employment locally. The area overflowed with churches, schools and public buildings.

Ardwick is first mentioned in 1283 as Atheriswyke or Aderwyk. The name is Anglo-Saxon and probably means 'Aethelred's wic', wic meaning a row of houses or homestead. The spelling changed over the years through Ardewike and Ardwyke to Ardwick. By 1522 there was Nether or Lower Ardwick, as opposed to Higher or Over Ardwick, referring to the terrace of the River Medlock between the river and Tipping Street. In 1322 there were eight houses with about 32 inhabitants. This rose steadily through the sixteenth and seventeenth centuries to 242 inhabitants in 47 houses in 1772. By 1801 the population had increased to 1,732, to 21,746 in 1861 and to 40,846 in 1901. By 1961, after house clearances, the population stood at just 16,659.

The boundaries of Ardwick are not easy to follow. To the north and north-west the River Medlock forms the border with Ancoats and with Manchester city for most of its course. Stockport Road forms Ardwick's south-west border with Chorlton-on-Medlock. On the south side Ardwick stretches over Hyde Road to Longsight and to the east it borders on Openshaw and West Gorton, where the Corn or Black Brook crosses its south-east corner near Hyde Road. The main roads out of Manchester city centre traverse the township from west to east along Ashton Old and Ashton New Roads, as well as along Hyde and Stockport Roads in the southern part of the town.

Today Ardwick lies in the parish and parliamentary borough of Manchester. Originally in the early thirteenth century the lands were held by the Lords of the Manor of Manchester, with Ardwick being a sub manor, like Gorton, Openshaw and Clayton, and relying on farming. In 1352 lands in Ardwick were leased to the Booth family. In 1636 the sub manor of Ardwick was sold to Samuel Birch of Openshaw, whose family rebuilt the Manor House north-west of the green in 1728. In 1838 Ardwick along with several townships became part of the newly incorporated city of Manchester, within a ward with Beswick and with the town's own Thomas

Potter as first Mayor of Manchester. Kennedy describes Ardwick as being 'part of the inner ring of towns that long ago surrendered their identity to Manchester, keeping their names but becoming postal districts'.

Ardwick is almost certainly Manchester's oldest residential suburb with the rich and fashionable, especially wealthy cotton merchants, flocking to live around Ardwick Green in the early nineteenth century, with easy access to the city along the main roads. Originally perhaps a village green, the green was traversed by a long 'leech-shaped' canal of water. Its well-maintained gardens were railed off and reserved for the use of the local residents, who each had a key to the gates. Manchester acquired this green for its first public park in 1867, laying it out with three circular ponds, flower beds, fountains, a bandstand and seating. Fields stretched from the green northwards to the River Medlock and southwards to the area of Oxford Road. Ardwick Green North and the Polygon off Stockport Road housed people such as John Rylands, William Fairbairn, Revd William Gaskell, George Wilson and John Dancer. The Hyde family lived in Ardwick House, later to become Ardwick Hall, when owned by John Kennedy.

Tucked in between the River Medlock and the green, industry began to develop, utilising the water of the river, natural wells and springs. Heavy industries of all sorts sprung up, including cotton mills, lime extraction, brick works, breweries, iron works, bleachers and dyers, rubber works and firms servicing cotton and hat manufacturers. Shaw describes 'East Ardwick… as given over pre-eminently to Vulcan, who manifests himself by day in a pillar of cloud and by night in furnace fires…'.

The workforce to man these industries were housed in rows of terraced housing packed in nearby, and stretching down to the green. Engels describes two-thirds of Ardwick as being working-class by 1845. Shops lined the main roads. The upper class fled further afield to places like Victoria Park and the green itself began to deteriorate. The back-to-back houses with their primitive sanitation and cellar dwellings were swept away in the 1960s and 1970s and the population was moved out. Blocks of flats followed like Fort Ardwick but were unsuccessful.

Ardwick had also become a vast network of railway lines running from the north-west to the south-east across the town with vast railway sidings on the east side. The network of main roads through the town was serviced by the tram depot on Hyde Road, which later became the bus depot. In the twentieth century the town was also a centre for entertainment with a music hall, four cinemas, roller skating rink and huge billiards hall. Numerous churches of all denominations and schools served the area, as did public houses and swimming baths. Manchester City football club was started behind an Ardwick public house. Two volunteer army units had their headquarters near the green.

A decreasing population forced many of these facilities to move or to close down. Nowadays it is difficult to imagine how genteel and beautiful a place Ardwick once was. This collection of photographs shows how important and bustling a township Ardwick was. Many of the photographs come from the family albums of people who loved their town and were forced out in the clearances. It is thanks to people like Les Sutton that much of the town's history has been recorded.

One
Around Ardwick Green

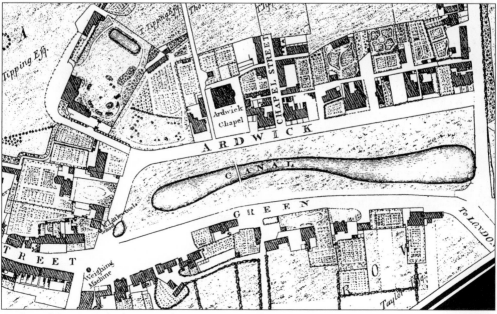

A plan of the green looking north, 1793. Originally probably the village green and first referred to as 'Ardwick Green' in 1685, it became a privately owned open space for the residents. By the 1820s it was fenced off with residents having keys for access and paying a small annual fee of 2s 6d a quarter so that men could be hired to maintain the grounds. Passing on the keys to somebody else incurred a fine. The 'leech shaped' lake, known as the 'canal' stretched along the green with a footbridge opposite St Thomas's church.

Ardwick Green looking west, 1915. The long waterway was partially filled in. In 1867 Manchester City Council acquired the green for £2,068 as their first public park, renaming it 'Ardwick Green Park' and creating ponds with fountains and the bandstand in the distance. Here was the setting for the accident on the ice in *The Manchester Man* by Mrs Linnaeus Banks in 1896. In the distance on the left are the Volunteers' Barracks (see p. 52) next to the chimney and tower of Jewsbury and Brown's mineral works (see pp 67-8), with St Thomas's tower on the extreme right.

Ardwick Green looking north-west, *c.* 1900. The house left of St Thomas's church still stands, whereas those on the right of the church do not. The annual fee payable by residents fronting the green rose to 10s and later to £1. John Kennedy of nearby Ardwick Hall was responsible for maintaining the green for a period. As the increasing rows of terraced houses encroached on the elegant homes around the green the local children with their 'infectious and contagious' diseases were harder to keep out of the park.

City of Manchester.   **Chorlton Union.**

TOWNSHIP OF SOUTH MANCHESTER.

POOR RATE, 1904-1905.—Due on Demand.

ST. LUKE'S DISTRICT No. 2.

Mr. J. BIRCH, Collector.—Attends at Ardwick Town Hall, Thursdays, 9 to 4.

M *E. J. Walker*

The Overseers of the Poor demand payment of the Poor Rate made the 24th day of June, 1904, to meet expenses which will be incurred before the 24th day of June, 1905, now due from you in respect of the hereditaments of which the Assessment Nos. and Rateable Value are stated hereon.

Poor Rate, 8/2 in the £.

Assessment No.	DESCRIPTION OF PROPERTY. Buildings and other hereditaments, not being Agricultural Land.	Rateable Value.	Amount of Rate at 4s. 1d. in the £ on Agricultural Land, and at 8s. 2d. in the £ on other Hereditaments.			Allowance of 20 o/o to be made to Owners who agree in writing to, and do, by the 29th Sept., 1904, pay the current Rate on all their Hereditaments assessed at and under £10.			Net Amount of Rate, subject to the conditions specified in column 5.		
1	2	3	4			5			6		
		£	s.	£	s.	d.	£	s.	d.	£	s.	d.
30 9 5¹⁄₃	15/17 & H. Bishop Wesley 2¹	25	5	10	6	2	2	1	2	8	5	·
32 2 6 5⁷⁵⁄₄₁	27, Jell 2¹.	90	15	37	1	1	7	8	2	29	12	11
3 2 2 7⁷⁵⁄₈₈	34 —	79	10	32	9	3	6	9	11	25	19	4

An official form used by Ardwick Town Hall, 1904-1905. By the end of the nineteenth century the green had become 'the focus of local community services' with the Town Hall, postal services, nurses' home, dispensary and Industrial school on Ardwick Green North. The Town Hall at No. 26 had been converted from a private residence. Broad stone steps, flanked by ornamental lamps, led up to mahogany doors set in a stone pedestal. The spacious entrance hall had marbled pillars from which a broad, fine stairway led upwards.

John Rylands, cotton merchant, known as a 'merchant prince' or Manchester's first multi-millionaire and resident at No. 24 Ardwick Green North from 1850 until 1855. On his remarriage he moved from Gorton Villa into Ardwick and then to Longford Hall in Stretford. The next door residence became Ardwick Town Hall and by the 1870s his own home had become one of three used by the Northern Counties Hospital for Incurables. His wife Enriqueta commissioned the John Reynolds Library in Deansgate as his tribute in the 1890s.

Saturday in Ardwick Green, 1889. The green, thronged by families enjoying the open air in the park, was once a private railed-off area for the residents, then a public park with circular ponds. A shelter can be seen on the left and also the tower of the parish church of St Thomas, which today still dominates the scene on the north side, although now no longer functioning as a church.

St Thomas's church on Ardwick Green North, c. 1900. Right was the Birch Endowed school of 1754, replaced by a church school in the nineteenth century, which itself was replaced by another school behind the church in the 1870s. The former was part of Canon Wray's cottages of 1822, two small and one larger cottage, which had its west, ivy-clad gable in the graveyard, buttressed onto an alleyway. On the left is No. 31 Ardwick Green North, separated from the church by Thirsk (until 1945 Thomas) Street.

12

Number 31 Ardwick Green North lying on the west side of St Thomas's church and divided from it by Thirsk (once Thomas) Street, now a passageway. Presently empty, originally this fine house, built in 1741 by Hayley, was a private residence overlooking the green and is probably the home of the Aspinall family as described in *The Manchester Man*. This house was once home to the employees of the firm of Affleck and Brown and also to the Initial Towel Supply Co.

The corner of Manor Street on the left and the west end of Ardwick Green North. On the right is the newer two-storey rectory of St Thomas's church. Centre is No. 29, once the rectory of St Thomas's church, and on the left No. 27, which later became Tom Dobbins' Old People's Club. Tom's firm was nearby at the west end of the green (see p. 72). These houses first appear on a map of 1832 but prior to that were part of the grounds of Ardwick Manor House.

Numbers 21, 23, 25 and what was once the Grove hotel on Manor Street, viewed from the west side of Ardwick Green North. These houses first appear on a map of 1832. Tom Dobbins lived at No. 23 for many years and his firm was to the left of this photograph. The Grove Hotel stretched around the corner onto Ardwick Green North.

The corner of Manor Street, with a stone plaque announcing 'Ardwick Grove', leading from the green to Tipping Street, covers the grounds of Ardwick Manor House. Thomas Birch, a merchant, rebuilt the manor house for his family in 1728 and the downspout carried the inscription 'TEB 1730'. Probably the Tipping family, once lords of the manor, lived there originally. In 1882 behind Grove House there existed an old, low building five sash windows long with small panes and a low, old doorway, probably part of the manor house. John Dancer, the pioneer photographer, lived there in 1871.

14

The old urinals at the west end of the green, opposite the barracks, 1999. Some of the original Victorian tiling can still be seen on the underground toilets next door. The green had three sets of Victorian toilets. One set was at the opposite end of the green (see p. 17) and a third urinal was on the north side opposite Chapel (from 1955 Cotter) Street. Behind, the George and Dragon public house is just visible.

A view of the west side of the green in the early 1900s. On the left hand end of this block is Albert Buildings at the corner of Downing Street, in 1879 housing sewing machine, life assurance and china dealers, with a furniture dealer next door. In 1794 Mr Littlewood ran a school here. Centre are the barracks of the Ardwick Volunteers, including a sergeant major's house (see p. 52) and on the right the front entrance of Jewsbury & Brown's mineral waters manufactory (see pp 67-8).

The south side of the green, once lined with the houses of the well-to-do and businesses, now has only the building of the George and Dragon public house (see p. 103), bordering Hyde Road and Cresswell Street. Nearby in 1879, John Brookes ran a school, next to a coach proprietor. Further east lay Allerton Mount, home of the Mawson family and Mawson Street. On the green is the war memorial of the Ardwick Volunteers, listing their battle achievements (see p. 56).

A milestone still stands, set against the railings of the green on its south side facing Coral Street, declaring '11 miles to Wilmslow and 184 to London'. Once it stood on Oxford Road near the corner of Clarendon Street. Later it was built into a shop wall two doors away from Devonshire Street. Then it was stored in a yard in Trafford Street, Gaythorn, and now rests here.

The public toilets at the south-east corner of Ardwick Green, just prior to demolition, 1999. The ladies toilets on the left, with the men's urinals on the right, were the only ladies' conveniences at the green, although there were two more urinals for men on the west and north sides.

George Wilson, resident at Ardwick Green in the mid-1800s. From 1841 until 1845 he was chairman of the Anti-Corn Law League, founded in 1837 to urge repeal of the corn laws and based in Newall's Buildings on Market Street in Manchester. He was also chairman of the Lancashire and Yorkshire railway company, as well as being partly responsible for the construction of the original Free Trade Hall in the 1840s.

Ardwick Empire viewed from Ardwick Green, 1909. This fine landmark is rarely seen from this angle and shows how grand and important a theatre it was in the area. Private houses on Higher Ardwick are just visible on the left. By now the green was a public park with circular ponds like this with its central fountain and bird house. The shelter facing south and the plentiful benches facing the water provide seating and in the distance on the right is the south-east gateway into the park. A favourite sight is still a giant boulder, supposedly from a meteorite.

The Ardwick Empire on the corner of Hyde Road and Higher Ardwick on the left, *c.* 1900. This later became one of four cinemas near the green, after conversion from a music hall, renamed the Hippodrome in 1912. On the left was to stand the Coliseum picture house from 1912 until 1949, converted from a skating rink. Beyond the theatre on the left are large private houses and the spire of Higher Ardwick Primitive Methodist church (see p. 113).

Ardwick Hall on the right off Hyde Road and near Ardwick Green with Dolphin Street on the left. The original style Georgian House was built for Nathan Hyde by Joshua Marriott in the late 1700s with grounds stretching across Hyde Road. The family was connected with the Hydes of Denton, Haughton and Hyde and the Hyde Clarkes of America.

A view along Dolphin Street off Higher Ardwick in the early 1900s. On the right is Ardwick Hall, site of the Hyde family home. Around 1820 Ardwick House was sold to John Kennedy (1769-1855), partner in the cotton firm of McConnel & Kennedy of Ancoats, who refashioned the house and probably renamed it Ardwick Hall. On the left still stands an impressive works on Dolphin Street.

Members of Higher Ardwick Methodist Sunday school take part in the Whit Walks in the late 1950s. On their left is Ardwick Green as they proceed along Higher Ardwick past Dolphin House towards the roundabout at the green. The Union public house is in the distance and behind the lorry lie their church and Sunday school. At the front are Jillian Swindells on the left and Julia Andrews.

Housing on Higher Ardwick at the corner of Harkness (until 1958 Park) Street opposite the east end of the green. On the far left is the Union inn where Higher Ardwick curves to the east. Nearer is the converted building of Higher Ardwick school and minister's house... once adjoining the Primitive Methodist church. The house on the right is Dolphin House, which appears on a plan of 1849.

Dolphin House on Higher Ardwick near the corner of Harkness (once Park) Street, with blue dolphins adorning the twisting stairway. Its name probably originates from John Kennedy's crest, the dolphin. Annoyed that he had to pay tax on his family crest, he had railings erected around Ardwick Hall, topped by hundreds of dolphins, after which Dolphin Street and its passageway onto Hyde Road, are named. John Kennedy also had rows of terraced housing erected between Hyde Road and Park (later Harkness) Street and between the green and Ardwick cemetery.

Harkness (formerly Park) Street at its junction with Higher Ardwick on the right, 1991. Dolphin House is on the right adjoining what at this time was Val's Hotel, comprising four houses on Park Street, which first appear on a plan of 1858. The gateway to Higher Ardwick Primitive Methodist church stands on the car park covering the site. Higher Ardwick, once lined with old, low standing houses and shops, was described in 1911 as having 'more old-fashioned houses flanked with lawn or garden'.

Members of Higher Ardwick Methodist church taking part in the Whit Walks in the late 1950s. They are standing in Park Street off Higher Ardwick in front of some of the Georgian houses, which still remain. On the left is Julia Andrews standing next to Jillian Swindells.

Alderman Stephen Chesters-Thompson JP, *c.* 1900. He took control of the Ardwick brewery after his uncle Thomas Chesters' death in 1872. Stephen came to Manchester in 1866 and lived first in a little cottage near Ardwick Town Hall before moving to Higher Ardwick. In 1879 he was elected onto the city council for Ardwick ward. Eventually he moved into a house he had built overlooking Rudyard Lake in Staffordshire.

ALDERMAN S. CHESTERS-THOMPSON, ESQ., J.P.
(From a Photograph by Mr. M. Guttenberg.)

One of the foundation stones on the left-hand corner of Ardwick Conservative Club. It reads that the stone was laid by William H. Houldsworth, Esquire, JP, on 27 July 1878. The inscription on the right-hand corner stone has sadly been obliterated. The initials ACC stand for Ardwick Conservative Club. Opposite in Elm Terrace, a row of Georgian houses on Higher Ardwick, lived Gilbert Waters Hyde of the Swan Vinegar brewery on Grey Street, off Hyde Road. His father, Charles Frederick Hyde ran Chesters Brewery in Ardwick (see p. 71).

Ardwick public hall and Conservative club on the corner of Higher Ardwick and Palfrey (until 1952 Park) Place. The design by the architects Slater and Kendall, shows a fine building with decorated mouldings, three stone lions and the date stone 1878. The top of the building was later altered, removing the dormer windows and railed decoration on the roof. On the right is the corner of Higher Ardwick Primitive Methodist school. Prior to 1878 the club, with a reading room, lay on the opposite side of the road at No. 41 Higher Ardwick.

One of three fine houses in Palfrey (Park) Place. First appearing on a map of 1838, now only two of the three houses are left. In 1878 No. 2 was occupied by a chapel keeper, No. 4 by a joiner and no. 6 by an oil merchant.

Two
Street Scenes

HYDE ROAD TRAM DEPOT, MANCHESTER.

A busy Hyde Road outside the tram depot, in the early 1900s. On the right is the archway entrance, flanked on the right by a row of shops. In the distance is the tower of Nicholls Ardwick Hospital. In the 1870s on the site had been a sawmill, stone and slate depot and iron foundry, owned by Bennett & Sons timber merchants. John Marsland Bennett was a benefactor of St Benedict's church (see pp 111-113).

Trams on the 37X and 37E route of Manchester Corporation tramways, turning at the junction of Downing (originally Ardwick) and Grosvenor Streets, May 1947. The 37X turns onto Downing Street to travel along Hyde Road through Gorton to Denton. Behind the tram cars on the right is the large store of the Manchester & Salford Equitable Co-operative Society. Here between Gaskin Street and Charlton Place the Co-op had a grocery and other departments together with a reading room and large hall. On the right on the opposite corner of Grosvenor Street was a branch of the Manchester & County bank. When the Mancunian Way was constructed in 1967, clearance took place and many shops and buildings were demolished.

Downing (originally Ardwick) Street running down to the bridge over the Medlock, in the early 1900s. Across the bridge is London Road with London Road (later Piccadilly) station in the distance. On the right is a tobacconist's on the south-west corner of Ardwick Green with the Manchester and Salford Co-operative store in the distance. On the left, on the corner of Rusholme Road, is the Minshull Arms public house, which closed in 1962.

Stockport Road with Brunswick Street off to the right, c. 1915. On the right is the triangular Georgian block of James Stewart & Sons just south-east of Ardwick Green (see p. 73). On the left is the Ardwick Victoria picture palace cinema on the corner of Hyde and Stockport Roads (see p. 94).

Shops along the south-west side of Stockport Road, 1991. On the left is Polygon Avenue and on the right Old Elm Street. The higher towered building in the centre has an archway, which led to Burton's cooperage, where barrels were made for the many breweries in the area (see p.68-71). In 1965 the shopkeepers included a tailor, fancy goods dealer, an outfitter, second-hand clothes dealer, butcher, costumier, greengrocer, motor-cycle dealer and painters.

A statue of Sir William Fairbairn, 1789-1874, resident at the Polygon off Stockport Road from around the late 1830s until his death. Coming to Manchester from Scotland around 1813, a millwright and engineer, by 1817 he was in partnership with James Lillie, building iron-framed fire-proof mills. He made early studies into the durability of cast iron and into 'metal fatigue'. From his Canal Street mill, Ancoats, he was involved in bridge building, steam engine construction and boiler making.

Stockport (formerly London) Road, looking south-east from Ardwick Green, near its junction with Devonshire Street, *c.* 1900. The left side of Stockport Road is in Ardwick and the right side in Chorlton-on-Medlock. On the right is the Octagon Congregational church bounded by Goldschmidt Street on the far side and Cavanagh (formerly Callender) Street on the near side. In the distance is the tower of Kay's Atlas brewery, later to become the Vinegar brewery.

29

Another view of Stockport Road taken from the same angle, *c.* 1900. On the right is the Stud Horse & Cattle Medicine Co. On the left is a row of shops, which in 1879 began with a tobacconist's, included a milliner, fruiterer, stationer, sewing machinist, bootmaker, tailor and draper and ended at Ardwick Terrace. The railings on the left form part of the Devonshire Arms public house, whose entrance was around the corner on Devonshire Street.

Stockport Road looking north-west towards Ardwick Green, *c.* 1900. On the right is Ardwick and on the left the Octagonal Congregational church in Chorlton-on-Medlock. On the right the original Devonshire Arms public house lies back from the main road just beyond the first row of shops.

Tramcar 313 travelling along Hyde Road towards Ardwick Green, c. 1900. It is passing the side of the Ardwick Empire music hall and the name 'Empire' is visible on the wall. On the far right is a glimpse of the billiard hall, a long, low building, which stretched from Dolphin Street through to Hyde Road (see p. 95).

The cobbled driveway of Ardwick Hall, now leading into a works, off Hyde Road. The curve of the once imposing entrance still exists, leading to the converted stables and coach house. After the Kennedy family had lived there from the 1820s until the early 1880s, the hall was bought by the Poor Protection and Rescue Society in 1890 for Franciscan nuns caring for thirty children. In 1927 the company Affleck & Brown bought and demolished it to use the site for a van and lorry park.

A stone plaque inscribed 'Hyde Place' and set in the wall on Hyde Road, near Ardwick Hall, whose gateway lies to the left. On the 1849 map, Hyde Place consisted of six houses, with small front gardens, extending to Dalberg (until 1956 Darley) Street. Originally they offered lodgings for performers at the Ardwick Empire theatre. In 1915 the row contained three boarding houses, some private housing and a school of dress-cutting.

Hyde Road looking east towards Gorton, c. 1889. On the left is Burgess Terrace, then Nicholls Street next to Nicholls Ardwick Hospital (see pp 122-3) on the corner of Devonshire Street North. Opposite is Devonshire Terrace, dating post-1849 and stretching from Devonshire Place to Tiverton Place. Next follow St Matthew's parish church, Devonshire Street, St Matthew's Board school, Annan Terrace and the United Free Methodist church, where now the Star Inn lies.

Ardwick cemetery, privately owned and opened in 1838 at a cost of £18,000. The eight-acre site was intended for Non-conformists but became a fashionable burial place for people of all denominations. Twin Grecian style stone buildings, the one on the right the lodge with the registrar's house and the other the mortuary chapel, flank the main gateway. By 1950 the fine tombs were neglected and overgrown. 6,500 tombstones had to be recorded and removed and three open wells filled in, before all the buildings were demolished in 1962 and the ground levelled.

The main entrance to the cemetery at the end of Ford Street with its stone gateposts, once holding iron gates. A 1966 plaque on Nicholls Field of Nicholls Hospital reads: 'This field was formerly Ardwick Cemetery, where between 1838 and 1950 the remains of over 80,000 persons were interred, including John Dalton scientist 1766-1844, Sir Thomas Potter first Mayor of Manchester 1773-1845, Ernest Jones the Chartist 1819-1869, Robert Hawthorne bugler 52nd Light Infantry, who won the Victoria Cross at Delhi in 1857, and many others of all walks of life, who served God and the City in their day and generation.'

A statue of Dr John Dalton, scientist, 1766-1844, completed in 1837 and now sited in Manchester Town Hall. John was buried in Ardwick cemetery on 12 August 1844 after his funeral cortège had processed from the Town Hall along the streets of Manchester past Ardwick Green and along Hyde Road to the cemetery. When the site was levelled in 1962 his tombstone was removed to lie by another statue of him outside John Dalton building, part of the Metropolitan University.

A painting of Sir Thomas Potter 1773-1845, who also was buried in Ardwick cemetery. After helping the city of Manchester to gain its Charter of Incorporation as a city in 1838, consequently he was created the first mayor of the city. In 1840 he was knighted. The Potters owned land in Ardwick from an early period.

The Hyde Road tram depot, c. 1905. This fine building, stretching along Hyde Road and to the left along Devonshire Street North, was a symbol of the large tram fleet run by Manchester City Corporation. The five-sided clock finished off the effect of this landmark in Ardwick, especially as just across Devonshire Street North (originally Summer Place) stood Nicholls Ardwick Hospital, with two churches lying nearby across Hyde Road. Opposite here had been Ardwick toll gate on the Manchester to Hyde turnpike road.

Hyde Road by the tram depot in the early 1900s. The depot was formally opened in 1905 to house 265 tram cars. The structure included cast-iron pillars, steel box-girders and iron roof trusses. On the right among the row of shops and houses is the Rose and Crown public house with a newsagent's shop on the corner of Slack Street. On the left is the archway entrance to the depot followed by a row of shops.

Hyde Road bus depot, 1980. After trams went out of service, the tram depot was rebuilt as a bus shed on the same site. The five-sided clock was replaced with a more modern one on the corner of Devonshire Street North, where Greater Manchester Transport had its administration office. On the right, on the corner of Devonshire Street, is the empty site where once stood St Matthew's parish church, demolished in 1975.

The interior yard of Hyde Road bus depot, showing a range of buses lined up in front of the bus shed, 1974. The complex at one time included an engineering shop, body shops, a saw mill and cabinetmaker's and paint, signwriter's and coach-trimming shops.

'Fort Ardwick' on Hyde Road opposite the Hyde Road bus depot, 1988. Completed in 1972, this vast complex of multi-storey deck flats created 537 homes after the clearance of terraced housing in the area of Gibson Street. There was no play area, just a vast area of grassland and very few shops. Coverdale Christian church lay at the east end of the site on Coverdale Crescent, near the Ardwick Empire public house, which opened around 1974 to commemorate the Ardwick Empire theatre and closed in 1990.

'Fort Ardwick' on Hyde Road, as it was dubbed by local people, viewed from the site of the newly demolished Ardwick Technical school on Devonshire Street, with the Star Inn on the left, 1991. The nickname came from 'the grey, grim, totally uninviting and totally forbidding' aspect of the complex. 'They really are a visual abomination.' People wanted to move because of the lack of facilities and soon 'a major architectural and environmental mistake' was demolished and now housing covers the site.

A milestone set in the wall by the railway bridge near Grey Street. Being part of the wall it has survived and indicates the boundary line between Gorton and Ardwick, just east of the railway bridge of the Manchester to Stockport line of originally the London and North Western railway company. The bridge was the scene of the Fenian incident (see pp 54-55).

The railway bridge passing over Hyde Road, looking towards Ardwick, in the early 1900s. In the distance beyond the bridge on the left stands the Railway public house (see p. 99), whereas nearer, before the adverts, is the boundary marker between Gorton and Ardwick. The bridge originally carried trains of the London and North Western railway company from Manchester to Stockport.

Two tram cars passing on Devonshire Street North at the side of the Hyde Road tram depot in the early 1900s. The clock of the tram depot is just visible above the trams. In the distance is Ardwick Municipal school on the site of the old St Matthew's Board school, at the corner of Devonshire Street and Hyde Road.

A sandwich bar set in an arch of the railway viaduct on Chancellor (until 1955 Chancery) Lane, 1999. Appropriately named Chancellor's after the street, the shop was originally a men's urinal and was sealed up in 1980.

A wedding party posing outside houses on Buxton (from 1952 Buxworth) Street, 1924. William Aikin the groom is seated centre with his new wife Dorothy (*née* Brown). On the left is William's sister-in-law Nellie and on the right her husband Walter Aikin. Buxton Street stretched from Temperance Street to Higher Ardwick.

Railway property near the steps to Ardwick station, opened in 1843, on Blind Lane, which is across the junction from Temperance Street but can be accessed only under the viaduct off Midland Street. Ardwick is criss-crossed by railway lines, mainly on viaducts, carrying different railway companies in and out of London Road, later Piccadilly station. Nearby were vast goods and mineral yards alongside the multiple tracks, together with an engine shed, weighbridge and electrical cranes of both the LMS and the LNER.

A view from Devonshire Street North in the 1950s. On the right running along the edge of the railway viaduct is Temperance Street by Ardwick Junction. The turning to the left is Higher Ardwick with a tobacconist's at its junction with Temperance Street. In the distance is the tower of St Andrew's church in Ancoats.

Members of the Casey and Topp family, dressed in best clothes for Whit Sunday, on the steps of the Topp's family home at 22 Chancery (from 1955 Chancellor) Lane, c. 1950. The house with its railings and large front window was once a dressmaker's shop and the cellars were originally inhabited. From the left at the front are Terence Casey, Pauline Topp and Kenneth Topp. In the middle are Joan Casey, Eileen Topp and Derek Casey. At the back is Frances Topp and at the front Bob their dog.

41

A group on Chancery Lane near the corner of John (from 1952 Jamiseon) Street, c. 1958. At the back from the left are Eddie Warburton and Terence Casey. In front are Kevin and John Power, grandsons of the Topps. Eddie made this bogey on wheels. Around 1961 the lane collapsed, leaving a large hole outside Nos 20, 22 and 24, opposite the King's Head public house. A gas main had buckled leaving a twenty feet crater, which took two weeks to repair.

Pin Mill Brow, Ardwick.

Tram car 32 on route 28 on Ashton Old Road, looking eastwards towards Openshaw, c. 1937. Pin Mill Brow turns off to the left with Pin Mill just off the corner of the photograph. Off to the right is Chancery (later Chancellor) Lane. Across Pin Mill Brow on Ashton Old Road comes Lyon Street followed by the George & Dragon public house and further on Ardwick Independent Labour Party social club.

42

Pin Mill on the north-west corner of Ashton Old Road with Pin Mill Brow running to the right. This was an early cotton mill with its tall chimney, boiler and engine house and offices (see p. 72). Pin Mill Brow runs northwards and down across the River Medlock and so into Ancoats. The area around the bridge has changed greatly with its old works and housing swept away around 1965.

Limekiln Lane on the left alongside the River Medlock, looking towards the bridge, prior to clearance, 1973. Ancoats bridge leads from Pin Mill Brow on the left across the river into Ancoats. On the right hand side of the bridge is the Bridge Inn (see pp 102-3). There are the remnants of the wharf by the river, as Limekiln Lane led to the Pin Mill iron forge and Limekiln Lane dyeworks, where there was a weir in the river and a reservoir for the works.

The bridge erected by Manchester Corporation in 1907 over the River Medlock at Boardman (from 1955 Baring) Street. This links the Ancoats and Ardwick sections of Mayfield. Therefore Mayfield station was in Ancoats but Mayfield swimming baths were in Ardwick. Previously Boardman Street was a cul-de-sac north of the river.

A view of the River Medlock, which forms for most part the boundary between Ardwick and Ancoats. On the right is the Ardwick side. The river was lined on both sides with mills and works, which depended on the water for their processes or for transport.

Tram car 529 travelling along Bennett Street, May 1935. This car was built for the Middleton Electric Traction company and acquired by Manchester Corporation in 1925. Modified, it was used on route 53 until 1930. Then most of these cars were scrapped, except for about six, which, were used for special duties, moving sand from the Bennett Street depot.

The interior of the Parcels depot of Manchester Corporation transport department on the north-west side of Bennett Street, 1961. This was sited near the railway arches at the Hyde Road end near Rostron Street.

The former entrance to Mayfield station on Fairfield Street with the Star & Garter public house on the left (see p. 104). Lying in the Ancoats area of Mayfield, it was opened in 1910 by the London & North Western railway company to serve the suburbs of Manchester. The station covers a large area bounded by Fairfield and Boardman Streets and the River Medlock. Lying just south of Piccadilly station, in 1946 it acted as an auxiliary station for London Road (later Piccadilly) station. Huge underground storerooms, housing bananas and other fruit, stretched underneath London Road station itself.

Mayfield baths on Boardman Street, lying near the bridge over the River Medlock, within the Ardwick area of Mayfield. Opened in July 1866, these were one of the earliest baths in the city of Manchester. Prior to that date bathers had to use the River Medlock. By 1927, 76,637 bathers were using the baths and 40,017 its adjacent wash-house. Damaged by the Blitz in 1940, the baths were eventually demolished and the site used as a Post Office depot yard.

The public wash-house on Birch Street in the 1920s. With its tall chimney stack it was a familiar sight before the mass production of domestic washing machines at an economic price. Other wash-houses were off Chancery Lane near the Wesleyan church on Dainton Street and at Armitage Street near the Marsland Hotel, where the female section became the 'public laundry'.

Housing in Crook (from 1955 Ragden) Street, 1897. Crook passageway in the foreground leads to Fairfield Street. In the distance are the steps leading to the footbridge over the River Medlock to Bung-Hole recreation ground. Opposite the steps is the turning into Raven Street. This area is right on the border of Ardwick and Ancoats with the river forming the boundary, as it passes under the recreation ground.

The back entry to Derby (from 1952 Dartford) Street and Ross Place, in the 1950s. Barbara Jones with Anthony Mason chats over the wall to Sheila Hough. The housing stretched between Hyde and Stockport Roads and from Whitfield to Coverdale Streets. The area was cleared in 1964.

Barbara Jones and Anthony Mason playing in the back entry of Derby (from 1956 Dwyer) Place in the early 1960s.

Ruth Ibram on the left with her in-law Dorothy Chadwick (*née* Ellison) on Bainbridge Street in the early 1960s. In the distance is housing on Aked Street, which was cleared in the 1970s.

Barber's wife, Mrs Gilberthorpe, stands with a lad and Albert Henshaw (right) on Grey Street facing the 'Sand' Park, *c.* 1937. South Street lies in front of them with Earl Street on the right. Wycliffe Street leads off Grey Street behind them, with the turning left to Gorton Street visible off it. Behind them also is the Grey Mare Inn. The park, officially called Grey Street park, was originally tram sheds and stables. Part of a shed became a shelter in the park.

Members of the Salvation Army's Goodwill Centre in Ardwick (see pp 116-7). They are helping residents to move from Gibson Street during house clearances in the 1960s. Gibson Street ran parallel with Hyde Road and 'Fort Ardwick' was built on the site in 1972 (see p. 37). In the distance on the right is Ardwick Technical High School. Many parts of Ardwick experienced house clearance schemes in the 1960s and 1970s, when rows of terraced housing were swept away and families displaced from Ardwick.

Three
Ardwick at War

A group of soldiers waiting for demob outside Belle Vue Pleasure Gardens, c. 1918. The signboard makes fun by reading 'Hunland, Way In. Belle Vue.' Bottom right is Alan Aikin's father, William, who worked at the Deansgate goods depot during the Second World War. The Aikins lived first at Garden and then at Gilmour Streets in Ardwick. Alan and two other brothers were evacuated during the Second World War.

The headquarters of The 1st Manchester Volunteer Battalion, formed in 1859, in the late 1880s. Designed by Lawrence Booth and built by the Manchester firm of Robert Neill & Co at a cost of about £8,500, from 1887 it has dominated the south-west end of Ardwick Green, near Downing Street. On the right is the building later used by Jewsbury & Brown (see pp 67-68) and on the left Albert Buildings, housing several shops.

The headquarters from 1889 of The 5th (Ardwick) Volunteer Battalion, The Manchester Regiment, in the 1890s. Between 1864 and 1894 the battalion grew from 928 to 1,148 men. The Volunteers saw distinguished action, including service during the Boer War at Ladysmith involving 112 officers and men. In 1908 another name change altered 'The 5th' to 'The 8th' infantry regiment. The headquarters included a house for the sergeant major, rooms for socialising, lectures and offices, as well as a drill hall and a fire-proof armoury with racks for 1,136 stands of arms.

The site of the headquarters of the 7th Lancashire Artillery Volunteers, later the 252, Field Regiment of the Royal Artillery of the Territorial Army, on the south side of Hyde Road, with the Apollo cinema on the right. First used in the late 1800s as the regiment's headquarters and drill hall, it had a war memorial in front of the Officers' Mess between Darley Street and the roundabout. The drill hall developed into a sports' centre offering indoor sports, large games hall, walled games enclosure, projectile range and even a dance hall with an adjacent licensed bar. During the Second World War it was destroyed by bombs (see pp 61-62).

The medals and tunic cuff of Ferdinand Stanley, 1818-1898, together with his memorial in St Benedict's church, recording his survival out of 600 soldiers in 'the Charge of the Light Brigade' during the Crimean War. He received these Crimean and Turkish medals, as well as four Good Conduct badges. As he was a worshipper at St Benedict's church, it was a fitting place to set his memorial, although his grave is in Weaste cemetery in Salford.

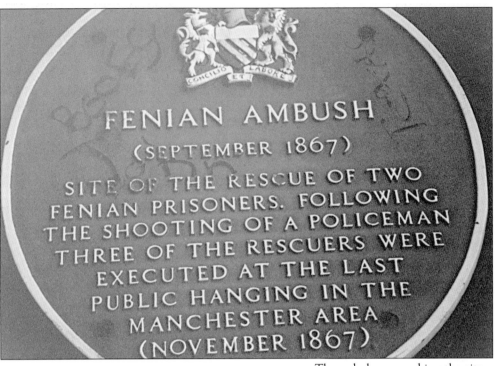

FENIAN AMBUSH
(SEPTEMBER 1867)
SITE OF THE RESCUE OF TWO FENIAN PRISONERS. FOLLOWING THE SHOOTING OF A POLICEMAN THREE OF THE RESCUERS WERE EXECUTED AT THE LAST PUBLIC HANGING IN THE MANCHESTER AREA (NOVEMBER 1867)

The red plaque marking the site of the 'Fenian Ambush' in 1867 on Hyde Road, just on the Ardwick side of the railway bridge. The problems in Northern Ireland came to Ardwick, when a police van carrying three Fenians along Hyde Road to Belle Vue Prison in Gorton was ambushed in a rescue attempt.

The policeman, Sergeant Brett, who was shot dead in the Fenian Ambush, during which two Fenian prisoners were rescued. Three of the ambushers were publicly hanged at Chorlton that same year, in what became the last public hanging in the city. Sergeant Brett was buried in Harpurhey cemetery and the Fenian monument is in Moston cemetery.

An artist's impression of the Fenians' attack at the railway bridge, where several people were wounded, some fatally, in 1867.

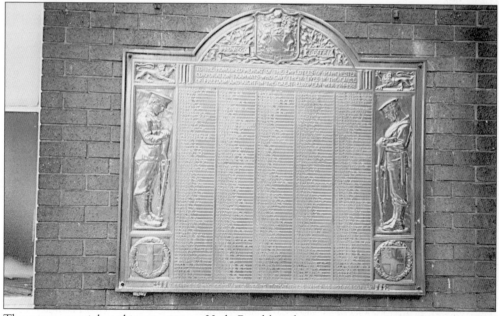

The war memorial at the entrance to Hyde Road bus depot, commemorating those who died during the Second World War of employees at the tram depot (see pp 35-36). The list of names is long and the plaque reads: 'To the honoured memory of the employees of Manchester Corporation Tramways, who gave their lives in the cause of freedom and fought in the Great European War 1914-1918.'

The war memorial at the west end of Ardwick Green of the 8th (Ardwick) Battalion, commemorating the regiment's battle honours in various wars The sides are headed by the names 'GALLIPOLI', 'EGYPT', 'FLANDERS' and 'FRANCE'. In the background In the background, the Volunteers' headquarters is visible. On this side is the badge of the 8th (Ardwick) Battalion Regiment, together with a memorial to their contribution during the Second World War.

Joan McDonald phoning to enquire about the progress of seven-year-old John Drummond. After the Ardwick Picture theatre was bombed in 1941, an emergency static water tank was installed on the site, at the side of the Apollo cinema. Children often played there. Joan, aged nineteen, working at James Stewart & Sons saw John fall in, rushed across Stockport Road, jumped in and rescued him, watched by a crowd, which included his mother. The tank was removed shortly thereafter.

56

A group of children being evacuated from St Aloysius' church school to Mow Cop near Congleton, in autumn 1939. Most were to stay there until winter 1940 but after the 1940 Blitz they were re-evacuated to Church near Oswaldtwistle. One boy, Joe Agnew, aged ten and standing on the left at the front with his brother Jimmy and mother Edith and Katherine Leonard (*née* Corbett), remained at Mow Cop and became the village postmaster. He arranged a reunion for these evacuees fifty years on in 1989. With the children are their teachers and stewards.

The Aikin family just prior to evacuation. Top right is Harry aged ten next to William, who was not evacuated. Bottom left is Neville aged eight, next to Alan aged six. They assembled at St Thomas's school and were sent from Ardwick to Sudbury in Derbyshire with many other children, staying first at Sudbury Hall and then with farming families. One evacuee, George Walker, aged twelve, stayed on and settled at Burton.

I WAS A STRANGER — AND YOU LET ME IN

An eight foot high, stained glass window set in All Saints' church at Sudbury in Derbyshire, commissioned by and commemorating the evacuees there in the 1940s. The 'dove of peace' surmounts a girl and boy evacuee, each with their sparse luggage, a strong cardboard box containing a gas mask and with an identification label. Alan Aikin traced these evacuees and in June 2001 held a reunion at Sudbury to dedicate this window.

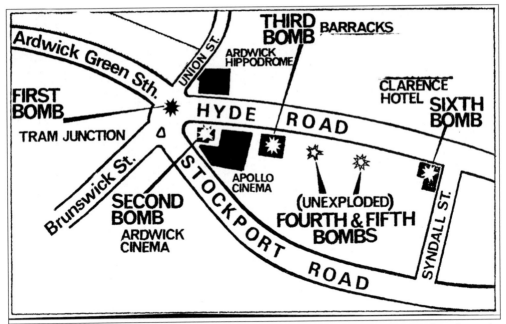

A map showing the damage caused by six bombs dropped on Ardwick during a raid on the night of 11 March 1941. The first one landed at the south-east corner of Ardwick Green and the others landed along Hyde Road, reaching 250 yards, as far as the corner of Syndall Street. The bombs were perhaps meant for London Road (later Piccadilly) station and the large goods yard at Mayfield station but the bomber was off-target.

The bomb crater caused by the first bomb, 1941. This is the junction of Brunswick Street and Hyde Road at the south-east corner of Ardwick Green, which is visible on the right hand side. Housing on the north side of the green is visible across the park. At this point, where the roundabout now lies, five sets of double tramlines converged at the green and may have confused the pilot.

The Ardwick Picture Theatre was destroyed with a direct hit by the second bomb in 1941. On the left is the edge of the Apollo cinema, which escaped unscathed. The picture theatre, just emptied of patrons, caught fire as a result of the bombing, had to be demolished and was never rebuilt. The cinema was showing the Gary Cooper film *The Westerner* that week and posters advertising the film were all that remained, flapping in the wind.

Territorial Army Headquarters on Hyde Road, destroyed by the third bomb, 1941. This was the home of the 7th Lancashire Artillery Volunteers, later the 252 Field Regiment of the Royal Artillery. The front of the building blew out, killing the sentry on duty and hurling the unit's war memorial across the road. On the right are Hyde Lodge and Dunham House.

The Ardwick Drill hall and headquarters on Hyde Road, destroyed by bombing, 1941. On the left is a terraced row of houses named Worsley Terrace. What survived the bomb went in the clearances of the 1960s.

Another view of the headquarters on Hyde Road destroyed by bombing, with the side wall of the building still standing among the debris, 1941. On the right Hyde Road leads on to Ardwick Green. Two other bombs fell on the terraced housing on the left but were unexploded. They were safely defused but it was three days before the residents could return to their homes.

The remains of the Clarence Hotel on the left on the corner of Hyde Road and Syndall Street, 1941. Although hit by the sixth bomb, it was repaired and carried on its business. Next door on the right is Ardwick public library. In 1866 a branch library was opened on Rusholme Road to be followed in 1888 by this reading room on the south side of Hyde Road in what had been the Primitive Methodist church.

A street party to celebrate VE Day, June 1946. Taking place in John (post-1952 Jamieson) Street, the party included families from Chancery Lane, which is visible in the distance. On the right is Mrs Topp standing opposite her daughters, Eileen, Helen and Frances. Standing first on the left is Winnie McMahon next to Mrs Royal. Sitting down second from the left is Lily Carson.

Four
Work and Trade

The Spring Water Bank works of the firm Tempest Booth, who produced gums and starches, off Ashton Old Road in the 1840s. They probably used water from underground and not from the River Medlock. Later they became Whittaker's gum and starch works, taking over the Victoria brewery as well and brewing beer. There were various such firms supporting the cotton and hat trades by producing the gums and starches needed in the processes.

The headed notepaper of Robinson & Kershaw, 1933. Situated at the Temple ironworks on Temple Street in Ardwick, below a loop of the River Medlock, they were engineers and bridge builders. During the Second World War they were official contractors to both the Admiralty and the War Office. Other iron works in Ardwick were Robert Blair on Bennett Street and Smedley's mantle and apron manufacturers also in Temple Street. As early as 1840 Pin Mill iron forge was producing castings for machine makers to turn into the finished machines for the cotton mills.

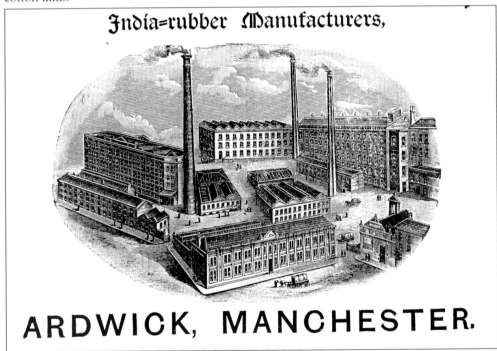

The Chapel Field works of David Moseley & Sons, 1901. Established in 1833, the firm moved to Ardwick in 1845, producing india-rubber, rubber gloves, rain wear, tobacco pouches and bladders for footballs and supplying flameproof rubber belting to the National Coal Board. These works were named after the area near Tipping Street, south of the River Medlock, in parts of which the firm had ancient fishing rights. They also had the Bond Street Works, where now the Mancunian Way passes, and the Medlock and Dolphin Street Works.

66

Jewsbury & Brown on the south-west side of Ardwick Green next to the Volunteers' Barracks. They moved to the green from Market Street in the city in 1890 to the corner of Grosvenor and Downing Streets, combining in this new building in 1892. Five storeys high and designed by Thomas Horsfield & Son, with up-to-date laboratories and machinery, the materials were red Ruabon brick with huge sandstone dressings in Tudor style. A 90 foot tower topped the south-west entrance with wrought iron gates at its base. After a fire in 1953 the top two floors had to be removed.

JEWSBURY & BROWN'S
SPARKLING TABLE WATERS
UNRIVALLED FOR PURITY & QUALITY.

FOR HOME AND EXPORT

SODA WATER.

SELTZER WATER.

POTASH WATER.

LITHIA WATER.

SIMPLE
AERATED WATER.

LEMONADE.

GINGER ALE.

QUININE TONIC

GINGER BEER.

HOREHOUND
BEER.

JEWSBURY & BROWN'S
ORIENTAL TOOTH PASTE.
White, Sound Teeth, Healthy Gums, and Pleasant Breath to Old Age.
CAUTION.—The only Genuine is JEWSBURY & BROWN'S.
PRICE, 1/6 and 2/6.   All Chemists.   Over 60 years in use.
113, Market St., & 44, Downing St., Manchester

An advertisement in 1889 for Jewsbury & Brown, showing that the firm still occupied two sites, in the city and by the green. They produced mineral waters, aerated drinks, Oriental toothpaste and brewed ginger beer. Hygiene and order were paramount. The water used had to be pure, its only contact being with pure tin and slate. The bottles were washed only in filtered water. Their lemon flavouring had to come from fresh fruit imported from Messina. Citric acid was specially crystallised in earthenware for them.

William Scott Brown, co-founder of the firm Jewsbury & Brown on Ardwick Green. Henry Jewsbury after his apprenticeship in a chemist's shop, set up by himself selling aerated drinks as well. He took on William as his apprentice and after his death William continued the firm. William took an active part in local politics, being first representative for the Collegiate Ward on the city council and then on St Luke's Ward in 1874 until he became an alderman.

An advertisement in 1956 for Slack & Cox brewery. The offices were at 1A Toll Bar Street and the brewery itself was on Hyde Road near the railway bridge.

JOSEPH BLEACKLEY,

SUN BREWERY.

SUPERIOR AMBER.
Pale and Bitter Ales and Porter,
SOLE AGENT FOR R. & J. WATKINS' DUBLIN STOUT,
ARDWICK. MANCHESTER.

An advert in 1851 for the Sun brewery. This appears on a map of 1794 and lay north of Ardwick (later Downing) Street at the lower end of Tipping Street. Joseph Bleackley owned it in its early days. The Britannia brewery on Broadie Street was founded in 1838 by William Nell, ceasing to trade around the 1920s. The Royal Hen & Chick brewery was near Ancoats Bridge in the 1840s. The Viaduct brewery operated from Viaduct Street from the 1880s. Yates Castle brewery was sited off Fairfield (once Ogden) Street and the Victoria was on Midland Street in the 1880s.

The site of the ice works of the Ryder family on Stove (later Baring) Street on the corner of Tipping Street, just below Mayfield baths (see p. 46). Beyond is the River Medlock and Ardwick's boundary with Ancoats. The brewers Collins & Chesters moved in from Audenshaw around 1869 leasing the building from Thomas Chesters. After moving to the Fairfield brewery behind the Bridge Inn in 1882, they used this building as stables until 1892. The distinctive tower was for hauling up the malt to enlist gravity in the brewing process.

The Hyde family, 1900. At the front from the left are Gilbert and Edward. At the back stand Anne and Fred. In the middle are Robert, Charles Frederick their father, Charles Albert, Emily their mother and Arthur. Charles Frederick joined Chester's brewery in 1888, becoming Head brewer in 1894. His son also worked there in the 1890s and three other sons worked in brewing at the Cornbrook, Swan and Welcome breweries.

The annual banquet of the North of England section of the Institute of Brewing held at the Midland Hotel in Manchester, 1932. Charles Frederick Hyde of Chesters brewery and his son Gilbert Waters Hyde of the Swan Vinegar brewery, Grey Street off Hyde Road, sit at the far right hand side. Fourth from the right in the back row is Tommy Hyde who was chairman that year.

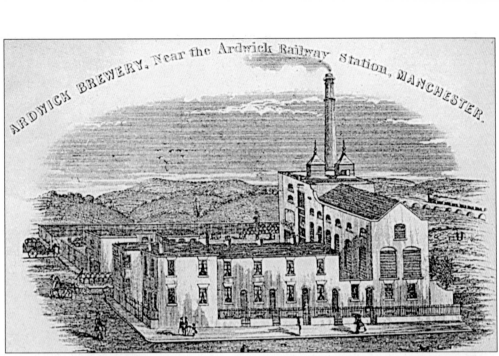

Ardwick brewery, 1851. The offices of Ardwick brewery still stand on the west side of Pittbrook (late Princess) Street. Thomas Chesters founded this brewery in 1851, utilising the stream along the street by culverting it and inserting a well. The brewery stretched between York (later Midland), Tempest, King and Princess Streets, lying on both sides of this street. After his death it became Chester's brewery company. This site closed in 1966.

Right: the yard of W. & J. Burton & Sons 'Ardwick Cooperage' at 60 Stockport Road. The arched entrance on the main road was set in a row of shops and led through to this yard (see p. 28). Left: the interior of a cooperage. The number of breweries in Ardwick naturally attracted coopers to the area.

TELEPHONES: 2575·6·7·ARDWICK·MANCHESTER
TELEGRAMS & CABLES:"FLAGSHIP·MANCHESTER"

BY APPOINTMENT TO H.M.THE KING

J.T. DOBBINS LTD
MANUFACTURERS MERCHANTS & SHIPPERS

SPECIALITIES: COTTON CLEANING WASTE·WHITE·COLOURED
& GREY·MANY QUALITIES TO OFFER IN EACH TYPE OF WASTE
HOUSE·FLANNEL & SPONGE CLOTHS·BUNTING·FLAGS OF
ALL NATIONS·DECORATIONS·LARGE STOCKS KEPT

CROWN MILLS · CHARLTON PLACE · ARDWICK GREEN
MANCHESTER·1   6th March 1951.

Messrs.Wm.Barker & Sons Ltd.,
Tanners & Curriers,   TD/ES
Otley.

The letterhead in 1951 of the firm J.T. Dobbins Ltd of Crown Mills at Ardwick Green. This fine building lay north of Jewsbury & Brown's mineral water works stretching through to Charlton Place. They were merchants and shippers of all kinds of materials but their speciality was producing flags and bunting world-wide. Their owner Tom Dobbins lived on Manor Street.

The ornate doorway to the offices of Pin Mill on the corner of Pin Mill Brow and Ashton Old Road. This three-storey mill with its tall chimney was a cotton mill with weaving sheds in the mid-nineteenth century. An earlier mill appears on a map of 1793 and produced pins and paper, giving its name to the road beside it. It fills a triangular site, lying between Pin Mill Brow, Ashton Old Road and Mayo and Fairfield Streets.

The 'island' site of the firm of J. Stewart & Sons Ltd bounded by Stockport Road and Brunswick and Polygon Streets (see p. 27). James rose from being an apprentice in the credit trade in the 1870s to getting his own 'round' selling clothes and bedding and then setting up this firm and moving here in 1907. By 1939 the firm employed 150 in their suit factory, had 54 travellers and 30 'inside' staff with a shop downstairs.

Standing from left to right, Gladys Starkie, Joan McDonald, Ivy Makin and Joyce Yearsley, outside their firm, James Stewart & Sons, c. 1949. The Apollo cinema is on the left. Joan once rescued a small boy from the water tank across the road (see p. 56). By 1980 the firm employed over 1,000 people with branches in Leeds and Shropshire but in 1989 the business closed down.

A group outside the firm of Thomas French, engineering firm, *c.* 1952. Bainbridge Street is on the left off Rose Grove. From the left are Mike Kinsey with Ted's daughter Sally, Ted Kinsey and a gentleman with Susan Kinsey, another of Ted's daughters.

An advertisement in 1931 for 'GUS' (Great Universal Stores). Affectionately known locally as 'Gusy's', this business was established on the west side of Devonshire Street North in 1917 with five and six-storey buildings stretching along the street towards the railway viaduct, overlooking Ardwick cemetery. Across the road lay vast railway yards.

Workers about to head off on a works' outing from GUS, stand outside the firm, *c*. 1947. They had various annual trips to Blackpool or Morecambe. In the front row is Nellie Pratt, second from the right, holding her handbag.

A window set in the entrance to the offices of GUS on the west side of Devonshire Street North. Formed from an ongoing business, they grew to become Britain's largest retail organisation in the mail order division. They expanded across the road, building three blocks of five, seven and five-storey buildings, using the vacant tram depot site.

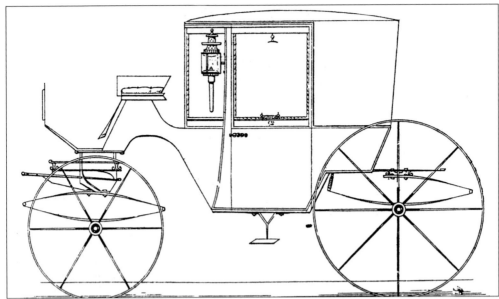

A product of W.H. Knibbs, coachbuilders, 1892. Founded in 1852 the firm grew to occupy three blocks of three-storey buildings, in a triangle around a yard, accessed by an archway on Tipping Street. The site included stables, timber and other stores with two floors devoted to coachbuilding, upholstery, trimming and painting. Hearses, coaches and carriages were among the many products. By 1965 Knibbs had adapted to become motor body builders on Blackfriars Road in Manchester.

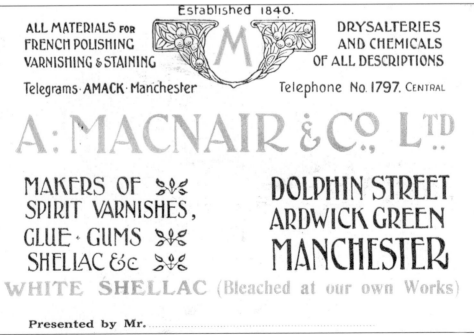

A calling card in the early 1900s of an agent of A. MacNair & Co. of Dolphin Street near Ardwick Green. Established in 1840, they produced all sorts of varnishes, glues, shellac and gums supporting the cotton and hat trades. They were also drysalters and produced chemicals, as well as materials for French polishing and staining.

The works once used by the firm of A. MacNair & Co. on the north side of Dolphin Street at its east end near Darley (from 1956 Dalberg) Street.

A Frost machine produced in 1892 by the Manchester Water Meter company, the sole makers of this positive water meter, supplying over 600,000 by 1965. Established in 1860, the firm lay between Tipping, Nether and Bond Streets, now hemmed in by the Mancunian Way, which destroyed much of this industrial area of Ardwick, which is penned in tightly to the north by the River Medlock.

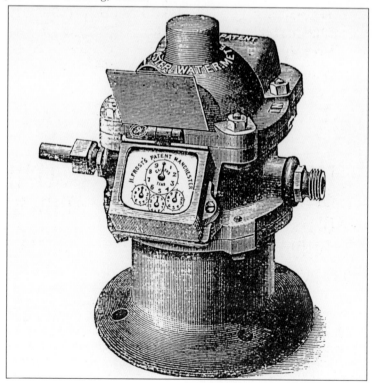

The interior of the Hyde Road tram depot of Manchester Corporation around the 1920s. New tram car sheds and repair workshops lay on Blucher Street off Hyde Road. Here trams were assembled, marshalled, cleaned, repaired and constructed. This made Ardwick a central part of the transport network by road and rail (see p. 40). A red and cream-coloured tram was made there called a 'Pilcher' and named after a general manager R.S. Pilcher. The last tram, No. 1007, passed through Manchester in January 1949.

Workers inside Hyde Road bus depot, 1959. On the left is a trolley bus parked over an inspection pit. The duckboards on the floor were to keep the men's feet dry and clean and a large coke stove kept them warm when they were at work in the pits. This group includes Derek Niel, Harry Cottrel and Henry Walker.

TELEPHONE Nº 3759 ARDWICK.

6. ARDWICK GREEN.

MANCHESTER *apl 7* 19

Bramhall park Golf Clu

Boᵀ. OF LOMAS & SLATER.

Sole Proprietor:-William Slater.

Millers & Corn Merchants.

ALL SACKS TO BE CHARGED AND NOT ALLOWED FOR UNTIL RETURNED.

rtilisers & Feeding Stuffs Act 1893 — the Feeding Stuffs named on this Invoice unless described as pure are a compound prepared from two or more substances or seeds.

The letterhead of Lomas & Slater of 6 Ardwick Green South, 1926. Their firm was on the corner of Kay and Downing Streets further on from the green and opposite the Manchester & Salford Equitable Co-operative stores. They were millers and corn merchants, here providing animal feed to Bramhall Park golf club.

Nellie Pratt, manageress, outside the Park House laundries at 273 Hyde Road, opposite Whitfield Street, in Ardwick in the late 1920s. In 1915 C. Shaw & Co. was the proprietor. By 1965 this was replaced at 247 Hyde Road by the Laundries Association, who were dyers and cleaners, near Marsland and Armitage Streets and Ardwick's border with West Gorton.

A branch of the Beswick Co-operative society on Ashton Old Road, Ardwick, stretching from the left between Claribel and Bellew Streets. Built in 1904 at a cost of £10,000, this huge building once housed a grocery, drapery, tailor, dressmaker, beef and pork butchers and a boots and shoes department, plus a vast assembly room and public hall. A ballroom upstairs was a favourite dance spot. The Beswick Co-operative, started in 1892, had ten branches by 1907 in Bradford, Openshaw, Ardwick and Ancoats with a membership of 7,000.

Rows of shops on Ashton Old Road, looking west towards the city centre, 1991. All this has been demolished, along with the rows of terraced housing behind. Only the Beswick Co-operative building and the Seven Stars public house in the distance before the railway bridge remain. In 1930 the shops housed from left to right the Co-op, chemist, stationer, hardware dealer, gentlemen's oufitter, confectioner, fried fish dealer and another confectioner.

An advert in 1926 for the Manchester Dairy Co. based at 53a Higher Ardwick with many branches, established in 1873 by James Boam and run in 1926 by his son. The lettering over the doorways reads 'Boam's Model Creamery'. The firm boasted how up-to-date it was, using costly machinery to ensure the purity of the milk and selecting farms and cattle carefully. Visitors were invited to inspect the premises. The dairy on Park (later Palfrey) Place on the corner of Higher Ardwick opposite the Conservative club later became 'Allied Dairies'.

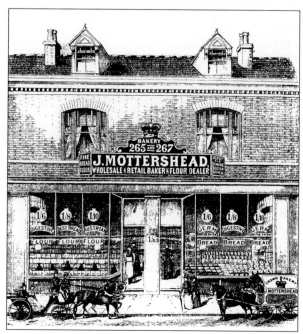

An advert in 1892 for J. Mottershead's Crown bakery on Hyde Road, Ardwick. This three-storey building housed its bakery in the basement with the shop and offices on the ground floor. Delivery vans supplied customers in the city and suburbs with bread, scones, rolls, biscuits, plum and seed cakes, confectionery, teas and jams. Another shop existed on Ashton Old Road.

The Motor Cycle Mart company on Hyde Road, Ardwick. This shop once lay next to the bus sheds, beginning life as a cycle shop.

Mazel Radio Service Station stretching from 122 to 138 London Road, Ardwick, between Brierley and Jackson Streets, 1980. Here gramophone records were sold, radios serviced and parts provided. The firm also had a depot on Rochdale Road. The row of shops has now been cleared but the skyscrapers of the university remain.

Five
Special Events and Leisure

A street party in Aked Street probably to celebrate the Coronation of Queen Elizabeth, 1953. In the distance is Ross Place school with Kershaw Street off to the left and the turning into Bainbridge Street on the right. Third from the right standing by the table and facing the camera is Ida Kinsey. Ardwick Market was nearby.

Another view of the street party in Aked Street, 1953. On the left is Aked Street and on the right Bainbridge Street. Ted Kinsey's wife, Ella, is standing at the left end of the right hand side table.

A street party to celebrate the Coronation of King George VI, 1937. The table is set out in Galloway Street, which stretched from Armitage to Bennett Streets, cutting across Marsland Street. At the front on the left sits Thelma Mottram. In the background is the works of Galloway's, boiler makers. Established in 1835 the firm was settled on Hyde Road by 1894, employing 800 people and producing a boiler a day. The firm won world-wide acclaim for their Galloway boiler.

A group of boys from St Matthew's parish church taking part in the Whit Walks in the early 1960s. Among them first on the right is Anthony Mason, aged six. Consecrated in 1868, designed by J.M. Taylor and built of stone in the Gothic style, the church led in the High Church revival in Manchester and was a favourite pulpit of Anglo-Catholic leaders.

The choir of St Matthew's parish church on the Whit Walks in the early 1960s. They are passing the terraced rows of housing near Nicholls Ardwick Hospital on Hyde Road. Second choir boy on the right is James Mason, aged seven. St Matthew's church was on the south-west corner of Hyde Road and Devonshire Street with its school opposite. The building was demolished in 1975.

A group from St Matthew's parish church taking part in the Whit Walks in the early 1960s. They are passing a row of shops on Hyde Road near the bus depot in Ardwick. On the left is the edge of the Motor Cycle Mart, next a hairdresser's salon, Thompson's signwriter's shop and then two houses. Shops and terraced housing used to line Hyde Road both in Ardwick and in West Gorton.

Members of Higher Ardwick Primitive Methodist Sunday school assembling for the Whit Walks outside their church on Park Street off Higher Ardwick in the late 1950s. Jillian Swindells stands on the right holding the ribbon.

Members of the Sunday school of Higher Ardwick Primitive Methodist church processing along Hyde Road on the Whit Walks in the late 1950s. They have just left Ardwick Green and are passing the site of Ardwick Hall with the building that once housed a billiards hall on the left.

Processing in the Whit Walks along Stockport Road, Ardwick, to Ardwick Green in the late 1950s. The Sunday school pupils are from Higher Ardwick Primitive Methodist church (see p. 113). The shop was Robinson's newsagent's on the corner of Apsley Grove with the Apollo cinema on the opposite corner of the Grove. Next to that shop in 1965 was a tobacconist's and then a baker's.

Members of St Aloysius' Roman Catholic church joining in the Catholic Whit Walks, 1949. Standing in Albert Square in front of the Albert Memorial in the city centre are Father Ernest Banks, parish curate from 1940 until 1950 on the left, next to Father Joseph Houston, parish priest.

Families from St Aloysius' Roman Catholic church process with their banner in the Whit Walks along Ardwick Green North in the early 1950s. They have just passed by the Church Inn public house and are walking by the graveyard of St Thomas's parish church with Ardwick Green lying on the right. In the background behind the Church Inn are blocks of flats.

Young ladies of St Aloysius' Roman Catholic church taking part in the Whit Walks and standing outside the factory of White's on Park Street, 1949. The firm made shirts and a sign in the window advertises 'Girls Wanted'. From the left are Chrissie Topp, Helen Topp, -?- , Edna Cronin, Molly Butler and Margaret Anderson.

The May Queen with her retinue in front of the altar in St Aloysius' Roman Catholic church, 1949. Seated in the middle is the May Queen Eileen Topp with the former May Queen Ann standing as her cushion bearer on the left.

The May Queen with her retinue in front of the altar in St Aloysius' Roman Catholic church, *c.* 1960. On the left is the cushion bearer, the former May Queen, Julia Goring next to the May Queen Frances O'Donald. At the front on the left is her page boy Kevin Power with the other page boys and train bearers.

A rare view of the Ardwick Imperial roller-skating rink, 1905. This took place in the building, which became the Coliseum cinema, next to the Ardwick Empire theatre on Higher Ardwick. The cinema opened in 1912 and closed down in 1949.

The Ardwick Empire theatre on the corner of Hyde Road on the right and Higher Ardwick. The music hall lay just north-east of the roundabout at Ardwick Green and was a famous landmark in the area. Opened in 1904 as a music hall and for pantomimes and seating 3,000, it was owned by the Manchester Hippodrome and Ardwick Empire company. In the 1920s films were shown occasionally and by 1930 the theatre was purely a cinema.

The Ardwick Empire theatre in the early 1900s. The tram is on Hyde Road and Higher Ardwick leads to the left alongside Ardwick Green. In 1935 the Manchester Hippodrome closed in the city and the name was transferred to the Ardwick Empire. During the war the theatre was sometimes host to the Hallé orchestra, which also performed at Belle Vue, as they were homeless after the bombing of the Free Trade Hall.

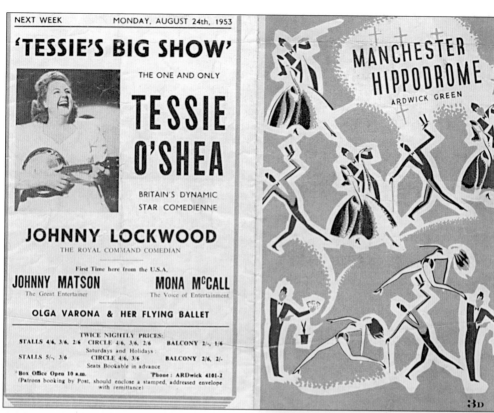

A programme cover for the New Manchester
Hippodrome near Ardwick Green, in
Coronation year 1953. The show was the
musical entertainment *Caps and Belles*,
including acts by Freddie Frinton, Julie
Andrews and the star billing Max Wall. Ticket
prices ranged from 5s in the stalls down to 1s
6d in the balcony and the programme cost 3d.

Another programme cover for the New
Manchester Hippodrome at Ardwick Green,
1958. This time the programme cost 4d and
the ticket range was from 5s down to 2s 6d.
The programme had changed to a continental
strip-tease show with other supporting acts to
be followed next month by a strip-tease peep
show. The Hippodrome closed down and was
later demolished in 1964.

On the left is a rare view of the Ardwick Victoria Picture Palace cinema on the corner of Hyde and Stockport Roads, next to Apsley Grove and the Empire Inn, *c.* 1915. Established in 1912, the cinema changed its name to the Ardwick Picture Theatre in 1920. Next door, the Apollo cinema was built in 1938, which survived the Second World War bombing but the Picture Theatre was destroyed in 1941(see p. 61). A static emergency water tank was then placed on the site (see p. 56).

The Manchester Apollo cinema on the corner of Hyde Road and its main entrance here on Stockport Road, with its foyer the width of the long frontage. The sole survivor of four cinemas around Ardwick Green, it was built in 1938, seating 3,000. This luxurious and palatial cinema with a vast auditiorium was L-shaped. It housed a dance hall and café on its Hyde Road side, which became a mini cinema and then a public house. Live shows, including The Beatles, were staged as well as films but the cinema side ceased in 1981.

The building that once housed a billiards hall, on Hyde Road, 1991. Stretching behind the sites of the Ardwick Empire and the Coliseum cinema through to Dolphin Place, this hall covered part of the grounds of Ardwick Hall. In operation before the Second World War, it was about the largest billiards hall in the country, having forty-two tables. It became a garage for Affleck & Brown's, then a furniture warehouse and a supermarket.

Ardwick Lads' and Mens' Club on Palmerston Street in Ancoats, 2001. Lying right on the border of Ardwick, this building was used by the club from 1892. Established in 1889 by Paul Schill and Will Melland, the club used various premises, including the two founders' print and finishing works and Mayfield Baths. Activities included reading, playing board games, gymnastics, camping, harriers, dancing, boxing and a Minstrels' group. Membership rose from 25 to 1,400

Busmen from the Hyde Road depot at a work's dinner at the Midland Hotel near Belle Vue, Gorton, in the 1950s. Seated are Colin (third from the left) and Irene Southworth, Bob and Mavis Comer, Jack and Bridget Hampson and Ken Smith.

A parochial dance for the members of St Aloysius' Roman Catholic church, December 1958. Held in aid of parish funds with tickets priced at 3s, the dance was held in the Palais Royal Irish club on Brunswick Street near the university. From the left are Sarah McDonald, Edna Cronin, Margaret Anderson, Ayleen Murphy, Margaret Hobson, Betty Lynch and Betty Topp. Behind the two Bettys stands Mary Cassidy.

Busmen from the Hyde Road depot in front of their special bus, which took them on a work's outing on a picnic to Blackpool in the 1950s. The outing was nicknamed the 'Tyre Men's Picnic'.

Busmen from the Hyde Road depot, outside the Half Way Arms public house at Bolton, on a work's day trip to Blackpool, 1954. The cost was around 12s a head, including all meals. From the left back row are Bernard Wolfenden, Les Fletcher, Henry Walker, Fred Ramsey, Don Preston (8th) and Ken Lee (12th). At the front are Danny Harper (3rd), Peter Ford (4th) and Fred Lowe(6th).

Machinists from Pin Mill on Pin Mill Brow on an outing to Blackpool, 1933. From the left are Minnie Duval, Margaret Weatherall, Mary Holland, Ethel Statham and Liza Barlow. Ethel was Frank Rhodes' mother.

Workers from James Stewart & Sons on a day trip to Blackpool, 1947. From the left at the back are Ivy Makin, Joyce Yearsley, Vera Morris and Barbara -?-. At the front are Joan McDonald and Margaret Todd.

A 'morning drive' for the regulars standing outside the Old House At Home public house in the 1960s. First licensed in 1828, the pub lay on Ashton Old Road just by the railway bridge, next to Houseley's motor body works on the corner of Wallworth Street, with the General Birch public house nearby. The Old House At Home was patronised by dancers from the nearby Lido ballroom.

The Railway Inn public house, which lay on the corner of Hyde Road and New Bank Street. This became a Threlfall's brewery house and lay near Ardwick's border with West Gorton, on the Ardwick side of the railway bridge. Beyond the bridge on the other side of Hyde Road lay the Junction Inn.

The family of the landlord of the Crown Hotel, Ardwick, when they were landlords at the King's Head public house in Denton, 1905. The landlord was named H. D'Alton Cleaver and his dog Chicks. The Crown was converted from a house and a very long flight of stairs led from the front door to the living quarters.

H. D'Alton Cleaver, landlord of the Crown Hotel, Ardwick, with his family at his new public house, the King's Head in Denton, 1910. The new Crown Hotel was demolished around 1974.

The Crown Hotel public house, at the junction of Chancery (from 1955 Chancellor) Lane and Fairfield (formerly Ogden) Street on the right, 1906. This was a Chester's brewery house. The Old Crown was opened around the 1840s and was newly built in 1898, when the lane was widened and the roadway passed through the vaults and lower rooms where once the cellars had been.

The Steam Engine public house just before demolition, 1991. It stood just by the railway arches on the corner of Birch (from 1951 Dainton) Street and on the right Higher Sheffield Street. In the background on the left is part of Ardwick Brewery on Princess Street (see p. 71). As a Chesters public house it would be supplied from this brewery.

101

The Apsley Cottage public house off Stockport Road in Apsley Grove on the corner of Sandall Street, just behind the Apollo cinema, 1991. In the distance on the left are firms on Dolphin Street and on the right is the rear of the Drill Hall on Hyde Road (see p. 53). First licensed in 1863, this building was probably part of the stables of one of the grand houses on Hyde Road, possibly of Ardwick View.

The side view of the Bridge Inn public house on Pin Mill Brow, 1973. Lying on the north side of the River Medlock across Ancoats Bridge, the pub really lay in Ancoats. Across the road on the left was the Ivy works producing shirts and blouses. Another Bridge Inn, opened in 1837, still lies just up Fairfield Street by the bridge there, behind which was the Fairfield brewery in Coronation Square. The brewery was demolished in the 1890s.

The Bridge Inn public house on Pin Mill
Brow, 1973. This was another Chesters'
brewery house. The sign on the right
reads 'Pin Mill Brow' and the one on the
left side says 'Ardwick Island'. The
'island' has now gone but housed a corn
mill in the middle of the River Medlock
with a weir and waterwheel.

The George and Dragon public house on
Ardwick Green South, just prior to
conversion, 2001. On the left is Cresswell
Street and once the pub was part of a row
of shops ending at Kale Street with a
bank. The original inn was a low, white-
washed building set back from the road
and demolished around 1871. The south
side of the green lies in Chorlton-on-
Medlock but is always regarded as part of
Ardwick. There was another George and
Dragon on Ashton Old Road in Ardwick,
whose original building dated from the
1700s and which had its own brew house,
closing down in 1968.

The Star and Garter public house at the entrance to Mayfield station on Fairfield Road and bounded by Travis Street. Built in 1877 the pub served customers using the railway.

Decoration on the Star and Garter public house on Fairfield Road. The building is finely decorated with stone mouldings, fancy brickwork and stained glass. The windows depict the symbol of the Star and Garter. The letters 'TC' on the building probably stand for 'Thomas Chester', who originally owned the Chester's brewery.

Three public houses on Hyde Road in the 1980s, now all closed down. On the left is the Bull's Head, next the Wellington Hotel and then the City Gates. Opposite the Bull's Head stood the Rose and Crown. In the distance is the railway bridge nicknamed 'The Fenian Arch' (see pp 54-55), beyond it the Junction Inn and before it on the opposite side of Hyde Road lay the Railway Inn. The public houses lost most of their clientele when the flats nicknamed 'Fort Ardwick' were demolished (see p. 37). The Bull's Head, which had its own concert room, was once part of a row of terraced housing and shops.

A group standing outside the Wellington Hotel public house on Hyde Road, in the 1970s. Part of the Hyde Road bus depot stretches behind it. At the side of the public house lay Blucher Street and the public house itself was part of a row of shops. The group includes Les Becket, Jim Mullaney, Jim Barber, Jim Burns and Ted Neillings.

The City Gates public house on Hyde Road, prior to demolition, 2001. Originally opened in the nineteenth century as the Hyde Road Hotel, this was the first meeting place of Ardwick football club in 1887, which had joined teams with West Gorton St Mark's church. The pub was renamed the City Gates in 1983 in honour of the side gates leading to the football ground. It closed in 1988.

A programme cover for Manchester City football team, 1952. In 1894 Ardwick football club reformed as Manchester City, used the Hyde Road Hotel as changing rooms and played on the field behind the pub, eventually having permanent stands. They played in front of Lloyd George and King George V, who entered the ground through the side gates beside the pub. In 1923 the club moved to Maine Road.

The team of Park Rangers football club, cup winners, winning 5-2, 1947. From the left at the back stand the league secretary, -?-, Syd Bibby, Peter Oates with the cup, Frank Caraher, Bromley Groome, Eric Perks and the manager Eddy Wagstaffe. At the front kneel Eddie Foley, Bernard Molvey, Robert Burns, James Burns and George Tatton.

A football team at the 'Sand Park' corner of Grey and Earl Streets in the 1940s. Among the lads are Bernard O'Driscoll, 'Spud' Murphy, Albert Henshaw and Ronnie Ellis. In the background is Yate's sewing machine shop, which produced shirts. 'Sand' Park was officially named Grey Street park.

Armitage Street school football team, 1948. From the left, front row: Joe Darby, Eddie Bradley, Eric Behena, Brian Ford and D. Dugdale. Standing behind: A. Jackson, Jim Dooley, Bill Parry, John Barnett, A. Lofthouse, Len Siderfin, A. Costello and A. Whittington. John Barnett went on to play in goal for Manchester Boys' team.

Six

At Church and in School

A wedding outside St Thomas's church on Ardwick Green North, August 1945. The groom is Robert Richie, aged twenty-one, in his naval uniform with his bride Margaret Leigh, aged nineteen. They were married from 55A Higher Ardwick. The church, founded in 1740 and extended in 1777, 1831 and 1836, was closed in 1978.

The parish room of St Thomas's behind the church on the north side of Niven (until 1968 North) Street. Established in 1906 and opened in 1907 at a cost of £2,000, the building lies east of Randerson Street with the church schools just across that street.

The boys' section of St Thomas's schools on Niven (formerly North) Street behind St Thomas's church. The first school was the Birch Endowed one next to the church in the eighteenth century. A second church school followed, lying east of the church across a passageway in the nineteenth century. This third school was built in 1870 for the boys, with sections for girls and infants following in 1872, separated by two internal playgrounds. The schools were closed in 1981.

A view of the exterior of St Benedict's church, 1920. Lying on Bennett Street and consecrated in 1880, it was funded by Alderman John Marsland Bennett and designed by J.S. Crowther. The brick structure is in the style of early Geometric Decorated and the bell tower soars to over 140 feet and was capped by a 10 foot high cross. The walls below ground are seven feet thick, five feet at ground level and two and three-quarter feet at the top: these are fortress proportions.

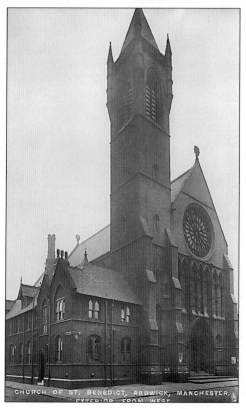

CHURCH OF ST. BENEDICT, ARDWICK, MANCHESTER.

The view looking from the west of the exterior of St Benedict' church, 1905. To the left runs Bennett Street with Dorset Street on the right. The church itself was part of a large complex with a war memorial, a rectory stretching alongside the church on Bennett Street and a parish room lying behind the church on the corner of Bennett and Gregory Streets. The cost was £30,000.

Alderman John Marsland Bennett, founder and benefactor of St Benedict's church, c. 1890. Born in 1817 at Summer Place in Ardwick, John took over his father's timber business, moving it in 1853 to land between Hyde Road, Devonshire and Armitage Streets, where later the tram depot would be. He lived first at Stratford Place on Devonshire Street and then on the Polygon. He also had streets built around the church named after his children, Guy, Jack, Gregory and Nellie.

CHURCH OF ST. BENEDICT, ARDWICK, MANCHESTER.

Members of St Benedict's church taking part in the patronal festival in July, c. 1920. The congregation made a procession of witness and thanksgiving round the parish on the Sunday nearest to the feast day. One priest, Revd J. Kitcat, during the time of the move against Anglo-Catholicism, hid the Blessed Sacrament but died before he could reveal its whereabouts. His ghost is said to haunt the area.

The interior of St Benedict's church, looking towards the high altar and chancel before alterations, 1917. This parish church in the High Anglo-Catholic tradition attracted worshippers from far afield. After 1970 the congregation fell from 5,000 to 800 and then to 150 by 1980 as the area saw house clearances and the population was moved out. The future of the building is now uncertain.

The Industrial school band in procession on the south-east corner of Ardwick Green with the spire of Higher Ardwick Primitive Methodist church in the distance, 1889. From small beginnings around 1820, this church moved in 1850 to a proper chapel and school on Ogden Street, nicknamed 'the Ogden' and finally to here in 1878. This was an important church for the 'Ranters' in Manchester. The church cost £7,000 but sadly closed in 1964 as the congregation dwindled in number. In 1980 the site became a car park but the school and minister's house were converted.

The interior of St Aloysius' Roman Catholic church, 1988. A mission church off Chancery Lane in 1838 was followed by a church and school opening in 1852 on Ogden Street. In 1885 this church followed on Park (later Harkness) Street off Ardwick Green, near the Primitive Methodist church. Falling numbers because of the house clearances in the area led to the closure of the church in 1988. The last Mass was presided over by Bishop Kelly and the parish priest Father Patrick Sanfey with a congregation of 600.

'The Agnesians' of St Aloysius' Roman Catholic church on Whit Friday in the school yard, 1956. These girls wearing red cloaks were aged fourteen and fifteen. Sixteen-year-olds called 'Aspirants' wore a green cloak and later became 'Children of Mary'.

114

Year One five-year-olds in the school yard of St Aloysius' church day school, 1944/5. The school was opened in 1904 further along Park Street, with an infants department opening in 1933 on Dolphin Street. In 1970 the schools moved all together to a new site at Stockport Road but falling numbers caused closure in 1983. The old school on Park Street became a refuge for the destitute, accommodating about 160 people a night.

A poster advertising a pageant at the Providence Mission at the Onward Hall on Lime Bank Street, 1925. This Temperance mission existed in the 1890s, had its peak in the 1920s and 1930s and closed in 1970. Its founder was James Armstrong. From shops in Ogden Street it moved to the top of Pin Mill Brow to the Ardwick Temperance Hall, then to South Street and finished up here for over fifty years, running various activities such as Guides and Scouts and a Prize Silver drum and flute band.

PROVIDENCE MISSION,
ONWARD HALL, LIME BANK STREET, ARDWICK.

A Grand PAGEANT
AND
CROWNING OF THE ROSE QUEEN,
Saturday next, June 13th, 1925.
Procession leaves the Hall at 3 p.m.   Returning at 5.30.   Crowning 6 p.m.

GRAND FANCY DRESS CARNIVAL
(Masked Dress Optional)
IN THE HALL at 7.30 p.m.
Parade for Judging at 8.0.   Un-mask at 9.0, when Prizes will be awarded.

Refreshments may be purchased at moderate charges.

Admission in the Evening 6d. ALL PAY.

Sunday, June 14th,
FLOWER SERVICE
At 6.30 p.m.
Gifts of Flowers will be thankfully received and afterwards sent to the Hospital.

GROCOCK & SON, Printers 44 Ashton Old Road Ardwick.

TIPPING STREET
CONGREGATIONAL
BAND OF HOPE.

A

PUBLIC MEETING

AND

ENTERTAINMENT

In connection with the above, will be held on

TUESDAY, FEBRUARY 21, 1882,

IN THE ABOVE SCHOOLS.

CHAIR TO BE TAKEN AT 7-30 P.M.

SONGS, SOLOS RECITATIONS, READINGS,
AND A DIALOGUE,

ENTITLED,

"WE CURED A DRUNKEN HUSBAND."

COLLECTION AT THE CLOSE TO DEFRAY EXPENSES.

A poster advertising the Band of Hope at Tipping Street Congregational church, 1882. This independent chapel lay on the north side of Tipping Street near New York (later Hoyle) Street. It ran from 1835 until it closed in 1882 when the building was declared unfit for use. Its members transferred to their Stockport Road church. Activities included this Band of Hope and schools.

Members of the Salvation Army with children who attended their mission, outside their Goodwill Mission at the corner of Gibson and Bunyan Streets, in the late 1950s. On the left is Captain Allsop and on the right Major McClay. The whole area was cleared in the mid-1960s (see p. 50).

Inside the Goodwill Mission of the Salvation Army on Gibson Street, in the early 1960s. On the left is Major McClay and on the right Captain Allsop. On the wall is a picture of their founder, General Booth. The first Manchester mission was established in neighbouring Ancoats in 1878 and the Manchester Divisional headquarters was briefly based at Ardwick Green in 1884, before it was moved to Swan Street in the city.

A rare advertisement for a seminary at Ardwick, 1825. There were many private schools in Ardwick, especially around the fashionable green. In the 1830s Butterworth tells us that there were in Ardwick ten Dame schools, eight common schools and ten superior, private or boarding schools, as well as two Sunday schools and the Birch Endowed school.

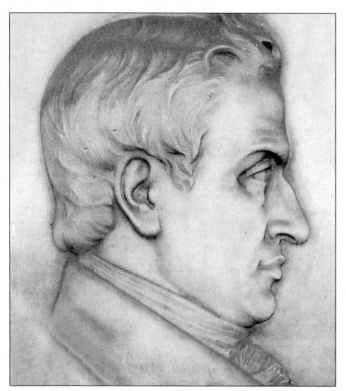

A bust of John Owens, a Manchester merchant, 1790-1846. He was educated at Ardwick at a private academy near the green. He amassed a fortune in the export/import business and left £96,000 to found Owen's College, which became the Victoria University of Manchester. He decreed that the college should be open to all men and so this enabled Dissenters to have a college education.

A class of seven and eight year olds outside Ross Place school, *c.* 1957. Seated is their headmaster, Mr Robinson with their class teacher. Behind the two adults stands Susan Kinsey.

A class at Ross Place school with their teacher Mrs Gaskell, celebrating the coronation of King George VI, 1937. Opened in 1881, the original building was demolished in 1974, when a smaller school was erected nearby. Among the boys are Ronnie Locket, Albert Jones, Billy Boyd, Steven Street and Brian Harrison. The girls include Marjorie Bell, Mary Shaw, Kathleen Pratt, Lillian Carter, Rene Ford, Joyce Blake and Joyce Adams.

A class of thirteen years olds at Armitage Street school, 1949. From the left, at the front: A. Jones, L. Bridge and Peter Ford. Second row: I. Bell, A. Lister, M. Chapman, the teacher Miss Bentley, S. Day, D. Sutton and S. Brogan. Third row: D. Bradly, E. Stappelton, B. Latham, E. Stoddard, Ray Millward, P. Hacket, J. McAvoy and K. Oakes. Fourth row: M. Loningon, J. Hewitt, D. Langstaff, M. Moors, B. Hutton, D. Preston, V. Ward and H. Boswell. In the back row are M. Cocking, M. Swinburn, M. Stott, R. Laverty, B. Wilkinson and B. Widdows.

Standards two and three at Armitage Street school with their teacher Miss Fletcher, in Coronation Year, 1937. From the left, front row: Eric Scrivener, Chris Finnigan, -?-, Norman Alexander, Bill Ford, -?-, Ronald Snelson. Second row: Norman Schofield, -?-, Bernard Snelson, Alan Rider, -?-, George Ibbertson and Ken Pickston. Third row: Bonny Shaw, Harold Ward, -?-, Sid Jones, -?-, Arthur Skerret, -?- , ? West, Derek Hains. Back row: Joe Bell, Albert Veiena, Arthur Fryers, Albert Fallows, -?-, Alf Stoddard, -?- Walker, -?-, James Hadfield. The school was opened in 1877, being the fifth school to be built by the Manchester School Board. In 1967 a replacement school opened in Gorton and the old building was demolished.

Nicholls Ardwick Hospital with Burgess Terrace on the left on Hyde Road, c. 1890. The terrace lay between Nicholls and Ford Streets, off which lay the main entrance to Ardwick cemetery. According to the inscription on the memorial stone, the school was 'erected in 1880 on adjacent land and was founded and endowed by Benjamin Nicholls and Sarah his wife for the training and education of poor boys of Manchester and as a memorial of their only son John Ashton Nicholls FRAS'. The boys had to come from 'honest, industrious and needy families of the Protestant persuasion'.

The front door to Nicholls Ardwick Hospital with the foundation date of 1879. This fine red brick building was designed by the well-known architect Thomas Worthington and modelled on Chetham's School in the city of Manchester. It was Worthington's last building and incorporated many decorative features from his unsuccessfully submitted design for Manchester Town Hall.

The tower surmounting the front entrance to Nicholls Ardwick Hospital with the motto *Semper Fidelis*, meaning 'Always Faithful'. The school, bounded by Ardwick cemetery behind, Summer Place (later Devonshire Street North), Hyde Road and Nicholls Street, included classrooms, dormitories and a master's house. In 1952 the boys were transferred to Chetham's School and the building was eventually bought by Manchester Education Committee. The name was later changed to Ellen Wilkinson High school and is now a sixth form centre.

The obelisk in the grounds of Nicholls Ardwick Hospital at the corner of Hyde Road and Devonshire Street North. Alderman Benjamin Nicholls, cotton manufacturer, was twice mayor of Manchester from 1853 until 1855 and this school was a memorial to his son John Ashton Nicholls, who died in 1859 aged thirty-six. This obelisk was also a memorial to him but set up by working men of the city for his 'untiring zeal and earnestness' in working for their betterment. His father died in 1877 aged eighty-six.

The memorial stone on the wall of Ardwick Higher Grade elementary school just prior to demolition, 1991. The school lay down Devonshire Street. The stone was laid in 1893 by Mr T. Thornhill Shann JP, a member of the School Board. In the basement were the gymnasium, dining room, science rooms and lecture theatre. On the first floor were a hall, classrooms and the headteacher's room. On the second floor were classrooms and art rooms. The playground area was very small with no playing fields and girls and boys had separate entrances.

Ardwick Higher Grade elementary school just prior to demolition, 1991. This was to become Ardwick Central in 1911 and then Ardwick Secondary Technical school in 1952. On the left, separated by a school yard, are the two parts of Ardwick Municipal school on the corner of Hyde Road. The schools were surrounded by rows of terraced housing.

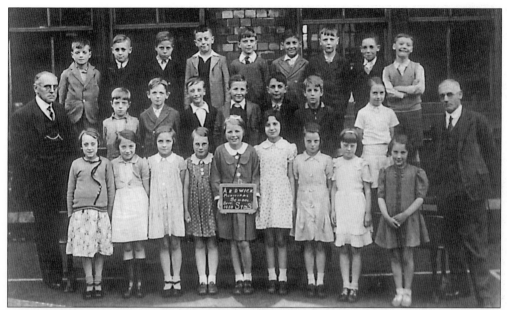

Standard three, with their teacher Mr Ball, on the right and headmaster, Mr Hillier, on the left, at Ardwick Municipal school, 1938. Standards one to three were classes for seven to ten years olds. This school lay on the corner of Hyde Road and Devonshire Street. In 1893 it had taken over from St Matthew's board school, which had functioned from 1870, catering for infants up to seniors. The Municipal school's motto was 'Knowledge is power'.

A class at Ardwick Municipal school, 1945. On the left is the headmaster, Mr Hillier, and on the right the class teacher Mr Bradshaw. In the front row first on the left is Alan Aikin aged around thirteen. Mr Hillier was head master from 1932 until he retired in 1949, when Mr Bradshaw took over. The top class had been evacuated to Congleton in 1939 and on reopening in 1940, as the ground floor was being used as an Air Raid Post, the school used the floor above, although many pupils remained at Congleton.

Prefects of Ardwick Municipal school, 1947. Seated first on the right in the second row is Alan Aikin aged around fifteen. The Higher Grade elementary school next door was overflowing with pupils in 1902 and about 200 students were moved out to form a new department called the Municipal school for ten to fourteen year olds in the original school with a hall, three classrooms and a cloakroom. In 1910 extensions were opened and three more classes added so that the school catered from eight until fourteen years old.

With the Hyde Road bus depot in the distance four girls from North Ardwick High secondary school for girls pose on Devonshire Street near their school in the early 1960s. From the left are Jillian Swindells, Sylvia Frost, Glenis Moss and Fiona Donaldson. Ardwick Higher Grade elementary became Ardwick Central in 1911. In 1952 it was split into three secondary schools: Nicholls school for boys in Nicholls Hospital, North Ardwick for girls in the Municipal school building and Ardwick Technical in the Higher Grade elementary building.

A school group at Ardwick Central school, 1933. This was a party of thirty-two boys, who went to visit Belgium, led by their headmaster William Peake and accompanied by teachers, Messrs Batterley, Dyson, Derbyshire and Muir. In the group is Les Sutton, whose three well researched books, entitled 'Mainly About Ardwick', are the main source for Ardwick's history. The group visited Bruges, Ostend and Brussels.

Demolition taking place at North Ardwick secondary school for girls on Devonshire Street, 1991. On the left is the original building of Ardwick Municipal school joined by a yard to the part in the process of demolition. All three school buildings along Devonshire Street were cleared.

Ardwick Technical high school just prior to demolition, 1991. Frank Rhodes went to school here. This was the original Higher Grade elementary school, which had gone through so many changes in name and use. The school motto was 'Duty First'. The school badge had a hand holding a torch and so the school magazine was called *The Torch*.

Acknowledgements

We should like to thank the following organisations and individuals for giving permission for these photographs to be included in this book. We have tried to locate everyone and apologise if anyone has been omitted.

Alan Aikin, Mrs Burns, Allan Crockford, Susan Hyde Fielding, Peter Ford, the Greater Manchester Police Museum, Gorton Library and Ken Lilley, John Heywood, the late Stan Horritt, the Director and Librarian of the John Rylands University Library of Manchester, Ida and Ted Kinsey, Katherine Lennard, the *Manchester Evening News*, Nora Mason, Chrissie Power, Neil Richardson, Margaret Ritchie, Joyce Robinson, Harry Shackleton, Colin Southworth, Stalybridge Local Studies Library, Isabel Swindells, Richard Wiseman and C.S. Young courtesy of A.K. Kirby.

Thanks are also due to Jean Marlor for the drawings.